Lady slipper

Blue jay

PARVA · SUB · INGENTI

Prince Edward Island at a Glance

Area: 2,184 square miles (5,657 square kilometers)

Population: 126,646

Languages: English, French (about 3 percent of the population speaks French)

Capital: Charlottetown

Entered Dominion of Canada: July 1, 1873

Provincial tree: Northern red oak

Provincial motto: *Parva sub ingenti* ("The small under the protection of the great")

Coat of arms: The upper third is a field of red on which there is a gold lion, the lower two-thirds is white, with one large and three small oaks in green

Provincial flower: Lady slipper

Provincial bird: Blue jay

Major economic activities: Agriculture, tourism, fisheries

Government: Parliamentary system with a single-house legislature called the House of Commons; 32 members are popularly elected to the House for terms of five years; the lieutenant governor is the formal head of the province, appointed by the federal government as the representative of the British crown; the premier and executive council are members of the House; four senators and four members of the House of Commons are elected to represent P.E.I. in the federal government in Ottawa

PRINCE EDWARD ISLAND

North Cape

Tignish

Cape Kildare

GULF OF
ST. LAWRENCE

Cascumpeque Bay

Malpeque Bay

West Point

Egmont Bay

Port Hill

Prince Edward Island
National Park

East Point

Elmira

Summerside

North Rustico

Bedeque Bay

Hunters River

ATLANTIC
OCEAN

Fort Amherst
National Historic Park

Georgetown

Charlottetown

Cardigan Bay

Vernon River

NEW
BRUNSWICK

*Hillsboro
Bay*

Murray River

Murray Head

Murray Harbour

NORTHUMBERLAND

STRAIT

NOVA SCOTIA

P.E.I.

CANADA

ATLANTIC
OCEAN

UNITED STATES

Provincial capital ★

Cities / Towns ●

Park ▲

Miles 10 20

0

10 20 30

Kilometers

sea to sea in 1885. On the map, the country looks square. But because the overwhelming majority of Canadians live within 100 miles (160 kilometers) of the U.S. border, in practical terms the nation is long and skinny. We are in fact an archipelago of population islands separated by implacable barriers—the angry ocean, three mountain walls, and the Canadian Shield, that vast desert of billion-year-old rock that sprawls over half the country, rich in mineral treasures, impossible for agriculture.

Canada's geography makes the country difficult to govern and explains our obsession with transportation and communication. The government has to be as involved in railways, airlines, and broadcasting networks as it is with social services such as universal medical care. Rugged individualism is not a Canadian quality. Given the environment, people long ago learned to work together for security.

It is ironic that the very bulwarks that separate us—the chiseled peaks of the Selkirk Mountains, the gnarled scarps north of Lake Superior, the ice-choked waters of the Northumberland Strait —should also be among our greatest attractions for tourists and artists. But if that is the paradox of Canada, it is also the glory.

Red soil, blue water, and the rich green fields of tidy farms make up the island's characteristic landscapes.

My Canada

by Pierre Berton

"Nobody knows my country," a great Canadian journalist, Bruce Hutchison, wrote almost half a century ago. It is still true. Most Americans, I think, see Canada as a pleasant vacationland and not much more. And yet we are the United States's greatest single commercial customer, and the United States is our largest customer.

Lacking a major movie industry, we have made no wide-screen epics to chronicle our triumphs and our tragedies. But then there has been little blood in our colonial past—no revolutions, no civil war, not even a wild west. Yet our history is crammed with remarkable men and women. I am thinking of Joshua Slocum, the first man to sail alone around the world, and Robert Henderson, the prospector who helped start the Klondike gold rush. I am thinking of some of our famous artists and writers— comedian Dan Aykroyd, novelists Margaret Atwood and Robertson Davies, such popular performers as Michael J. Fox, Anne Murray, Gordon Lightfoot, and k.d. lang, and hockey greats from Maurice Richard to Gordie Howe to Wayne Gretzky.

The real shape of Canada explains why our greatest epic has been the building of the Pacific Railway to unite the nation from

Contents

Cover: Green fields and sandy beaches on the northwest coast of Prince Edward Island
Opposite: Anne Shirley, the heroine of L. M. Montgomery's novel *Anne of Green Gables*

Chelsea House Publishers
EDITOR-IN-CHIEF: Remmel Nunn
MANAGING EDITOR: Karyn Gullen Browne
COPY CHIEF: Juliann Barbato
PICTURE EDITOR: Adrian G. Allen
ART DIRECTOR: Maria Epes
DEPUTY COPY CHIEF: Mark Rifkin
ASSISTANT ART DIRECTOR: Noreen Romano
MANUFACTURING MANAGER: Gerald Levine
SYSTEMS MANAGER: Lindsey Ottman
PRODUCTION MANAGER: Joseph Romano
PRODUCTION COORDINATOR: Marie Claire Cebrián

Let's Discover Canada
SENIOR EDITOR: Rebecca Stefoff

Staff for PRINCE EDWARD ISLAND
COPY EDITOR: Benson D. Simmonds
EDITORIAL ASSISTANT: Ian Wilker
PICTURE RESEARCHER: Nisa Rauschenberg
DESIGNER: Diana Blume

First Printing

1 3 5 7 9 8 6 4 2

Library of Congress Cataloging-in-Publication Data
LeVert, Suzanne.
    Let's discover Canada. Prince Edward Island/by Suzanne LeVert;
George Sheppard, general editor.
        p.   cm.
    Includes bibliographical references and index.
    Summary: Discusses the history, geography, and culture of the
Canadian province of Prince Edward Island.
    ISBN 0-7910-1023-6
1. Prince Edward Island—Juvenile literature. [1. Prince Edward Island.]
I. Sheppard, George C. B. II. Title.
F1047.4.L48   1991
071.7—dc20

90-46035
CIP
AC

Let's Discover Canada

PRINCE EDWARD ISLAND

by
Suzanne LeVert

George Sheppard
McMaster University
General Editor

CHELSEA HOUSE PUBLISHERS
New York   Philadelphia

The Land

Prince Edward Island (or P.E.I.) is the smallest province in Canada and also one of the most beautiful. Often called the Garden of Canada, Prince Edward Island is 2,184 square miles (5,657 square kilometers) of sandy dunes and beaches, saltwater lagoons, and some of the most productive farmland in the nation.

About 120 miles (193 kilometers) long and from 3 to 35 miles (5 to 56 kilometers) wide, Prince Edward Island represents just one-tenth of 1 percent of Canada's land area. Located in the Gulf of St. Lawrence off the southeast coast of New Brunswick, Prince Edward Island is one of three coastal provinces in southeastern Canada that are called the maritime provinces. (Maritime means "having to do with the ocean.") The other maritime provinces are Nova Scotia and New Brunswick. Prince Edward Island is separated from these neighboring provinces by a sea channel called the Northumberland Strait, which ranges in width from 9 to 25 miles (14 to 40 kilometers).

Although it is tiny compared with the bulk of Canada, Prince Edward Island has an impressive landscape. Its coastline is made up of countless coves and bays, high sandstone cliffs, and long,

Opposite: More than half of Prince Edward Island has been intensively cultivated for several centuries. The farms of the island's interior consist of gently rolling hills and shallow valleys.
Above: Near Cape Kildare in the northwest, the island's shoreline takes the form of rugged sandstone cliffs, colored red by iron oxide and carved into overhanging ledges by the relentless action of the waves.

sandy beaches. Deep inlets and saltwater marshes, enclosed by dunes, indent the coast. But fresh water is rare on the island. Only one lake and one river are fresh; the high tides of the sea carry salt water into all the other ponds and streams. The interior of the island is a pastoral landscape of low, rolling hills and gentle valleys.

Geology and the Elements

Prince Edward Island was created hundreds of thousands of years ago when soil from surrounding mountains was carried by the St. Lawrence River downstream into the Gulf of St. Lawrence. Then, during the most recent ice age, which ended about 10,000 years ago, the huge Wisconsin glacier covered the whole gulf area, and its weight compressed the rock and soil into sandstone. At that time, Prince Edward Island was still connected to the mainland, but when the glacier melted, the water rose to cover the connecting strip of land, thus forming the Northumberland Strait.

The glacier scraped away at the ancient rock beneath it, carving out the crescent shape of the island. Over the centuries, after the glacier disappeared, wind and water steadily eroded the rock, creating the sand that carpets the island's beaches and the soil of its farmlands. Visitors to Prince Edward Island often remark on the distinctive color of the soil, which is a vivid red because it contains a great deal of iron oxide from the ancient sandstone. Red soil, blue water, and green vegetation combine to form the colorful landscapes that are characteristic of the island.

The island's terrain is still evolving. Each year, the elements erode more and more sandstone, constantly adding to the soil cover. Although it is small, Prince Edward Island has a very high percentage of land suitable for farming. At the beginning of the 1990s, more than 50 percent of the island's surface was being productively farmed, and another 40 percent or so is considered potential farmland. Only in two hilly regions, one in the western part of the island and one in the southern, is the soil too thin for successful farming; similarly, a few marshlands in the west are too wet for agriculture.

Marram grass (foreground) helps to hold the island's sand dunes together. Here an inn sits on a knoll above a grassy landscape.

Red soil is one distinctive physical characteristic of the island. Another is its magnificent beaches—approximately 500 miles (800 kilometers) of them along the island's rugged coastline. On the north shore, facing the Gulf of St. Lawrence, the beaches are lined with towering wind-sculpted sand dunes, which are held in place by the long, strong roots of a tall plant called marram grass. Although they are a haven for beachcombers, when the dunes are shifted about by wind and wave, they can pose a hazard to fishermen, who need stable harbors.

When the first Europeans reached the island in the 16th century, they found a land covered with dense forests of hardwood and pine trees. Centuries of clearing the land for farming and of cutting timber for shipbuilding and construction have dramatically reduced the number and variety of trees on the island. Some species, including beech and white pine, have completely disappeared. Red maple, spruce, and balsam fir remain in scattered woodlands that cover about 595,000 acres (241,000 hectares) of the province. The caribou, moose, bear, and beaver populations that lived in the 16th-century forests have also disappeared. The island's wildlife now consists of small animals, such as squirrels and rabbits. But Prince Edward Island is rich in bird life, especially during spring and autumn, when many species of migrating birds pause on the island during their flights. More than 300 species of birds have been sighted on the island.

As the 20th century draws to a close, the people of Prince Edward Island are trying to conserve not only their remaining forests but the province's other natural resources as well. For example, although the island's soil is plentiful, some land has been farmed too often, draining the soil of nutrients. Farmers are experimenting with different crops and leaving their land unplanted

Each winter, icebreaking ships must clear a passage for sea traffic through the ice that clogs the Northumberland Strait and cuts Prince Edward Island off from the mainland.

during certain seasons to improve the soil's fertility. Soil erosion is also a problem, and the islanders are planting hedges to prevent it.

Another important priority is the preservation of the island's beauty. The islanders are faced with numerous opportunities to build hotels and resorts that would increase tourism, which is a crucial element in Prince Edward Island's economy, but they are hoping to avoid overdevelopment and overexploitation of their province's environmental and natural resources.

Climate and Weather

Prince Edward Island has a temperate climate. Although the winters are long, they are not extremely severe. Temperatures average about 20 degrees Fahrenheit (− 7 degrees Centigrade) in January, and the annual snowfall is about 113 inches (287 centimeters). Winter temperatures are cold enough to freeze the Northumberland Strait, closing off shipping and travel seaways to the island until special ships called icebreakers can clear them.

Summers are quite pleasant, with plenty of sunshine. Cool, moist air from the sea keeps daytime temperatures down to about 73° F (22.5° C) for most of the season. The beaches are popular with residents and tourists alike because the waters of both the Gulf of St. Lawrence and the Northumberland Strait are quite warm. Although it lies on the North Atlantic storm track and receives rainfall about one day out of three, Prince Edward Island is not plagued by the heavy, lingering fogs that frequently blanket the neighboring maritime provinces of New Brunswick and Nova Scotia.

The History

Long before the Europeans settled on the island and named it after Prince Edward of England, the island's earliest residents, the Micmac Indians, called it Abegweit, which means "cradled on the waves."

Some 10,000 years ago, before the Northumberland Strait was covered by water, wandering groups of Native Americans occasionally came to Prince Edward Island from what is now Nova Scotia to hunt, fish, and farm, especially during the summer, when the land was fertile and the waters warm. About 2,000 years ago, a small band of Micmac became the island's first permanent settlers. The Micmac are members of the Algonquian language group, which includes many Native American peoples in Canada, New England, and the Great Lakes region. They built villages in the interior and on the coast of Prince Edward Island and lived peacefully there until the Europeans arrived in the 16th century. In the following centuries, the Micmac were forced from their villages onto reserved lands, which are currently inhabited by some 400 Native Americans.

Above: The island's original inhabitants were the Micmac. This old photograph was probably taken at the Lennox Island Reserve, where most of Prince Edward Island's surviving Native American population still lives.
Opposite: Jacques Cartier was the first European known to have landed on Prince Edward Island. He claimed it for France in 1534, then went on to explore the St. Lawrence River.

Cartier and the French

Jacques Cartier, a young French explorer, landed at several spots on the north shore of Abegweit in 1534. He was quite impressed with what he saw, writing in his journal, "All this land is low and flat, the most delightful that may be seen." However, Cartier was disappointed by the lack of natural harbors. Not realizing he was on an island, Cartier did not explore further; if he had traveled around the island, he would have found a number of excellent harbors on the rocky southern coast.

After leaving Prince Edward Island, Cartier sailed down the St. Lawrence River to Quebec and Ontario. In the first half of the 17th century, these provinces became the first part of Canada to be permanently settled by European colonists; Prince Edward Island, which was named Ile St. Jean by the French, did not receive its first permanent European inhabitants until more than 100 years later.

In the meantime, however, France claimed the island as its own and granted fishing rights in the Gulf of St. Lawrence and along the Atlantic coast to a French trading firm called La Compagnie de la Nouvelle France in 1650. La Compagnie brought the fur trade and a number of missionaries to the mainland colonies but did not attempt to settle Ile St. Jean, using it instead as a fishing outpost. Only transient fishermen visited the island during the 1600s. The first permanent settlers built Port La Joye (later called Fort Amherst) on the island's southern shore in 1719.

The Neutral French of Acadia

Ile St. Jean was part of a large region that the French called Acadie, or Acadia. This large, ill-defined territory also included New Brunswick, southeastern Quebec, eastern Maine, and the area that makes up present-day Nova Scotia. The British contested France's control over Acadia and referred to the region as Nova Scotia, or New Scotland.

The first settlers in Acadia, mostly French Catholics and a few Protestants from Great Britain, were fiercely independent.

Artworks such as this drawing and poems such as Henry Wadsworth Longfellow's *Evangeline* have commemorated the distress and suffering of the Acadians who were forced out of their homes by the British. Some Acadians managed to remain on Prince Edward Island by hiding from the British for many years.

Samuel Holland divided the island into three counties and then subdivided the counties into townships that were awarded to British landlords by lottery.

The rugged landscape of Acadia, the long, cold winters, and the isolation from Europe and from other New World colonies helped to forge a bond among the settlers. These colonists developed a new sense of identity. They stopped identifying themselves with their native countries and began calling themselves Acadians.

The Acadians were determined to remain independent from both France and Great Britain. Furs, farmland, and timber, however, made their territory far too valuable for the great powers to allow it to remain neutral. Many times during the late 17th and early 18th centuries, Acadia passed from French to British control and back again to French. Unfortunately for Acadians, most of whom were of French descent, the British eventually gained the upper hand. The British deeply distrusted the Acadians' claim of neutrality and, in the early 18th century, forcibly expelled some Acadians from the area that became present-day Nova Scotia. Another 5,000 Acadians were forced to leave Nova Scotia in 1755. Some of them chose to flee to Ile St. Jean.

The island offered a refuge to Acadians who had been driven out of their homes in 1755, but prior to that it had attracted few other settlers. A French nobleman named Louis de la Port, Sieur de Louvigny of Quebec, was granted control of the island in 1710, but he failed to develop a colony there. In 1716 the chance to develop the island went to the Comte de Saint Pierre, a nobleman of the court of Louis XV. He too failed. A third Frenchman, Jean Pierre de Roma, had a little more luck. He built farms, roads, a forge, and other small businesses, which did attract pioneers from France to the island. Nevertheless, most people who came to Ile St. Jean arrived there from other parts of Acadia until the British gained permanent control of the island in 1758.

With brutal resolve, the British set out to expel all the Acadians from Isle St. John, as it was now called. As they had done in Nova Scotia and elsewhere in Acadia, the British rounded up the French farmers and fishermen and sent most of them back to Europe. Many of the Acadians, however, escaped to other parts of North America. Some of them eventually settled in Louisiana, where their descendants are called Cajuns. But about 30

William Patterson's zeal for land reform turned the absentee landlords against him and in the 1780s finally cost him his post as governor of Prince Edward Island.

Acadian families managed to remain on the island, hiding for years in the woods from the British authorities. These brave settlers were the ancestors of the island's current Acadian population of about 10,000.

British Settlement

The British had as much trouble settling the island as the French had had. In 1764, the British sent Captain Samuel Holland to survey Isle St. John and provide the Crown with a detailed map of it. Holland divided the island into three counties, which were subdivided into parishes and townships. He named the easternmost section of the island Kings County and founded the town of Georgetown, named after King George III of Great Britain, as its capital. The central part of the island was named Queens County, and its capital was Charlottetown. The western part of the island was named Prince County, after the Prince of Wales; its capital was Princetown. Princetown later disappeared, and Georgetown has never been more than a small village, but Charlottetown became the capital of the entire province.

Holland divided the land in these three counties into 67 townships of about 20,000 acres (8,100 hectares) each. The townships were raffled off to prominent Englishmen in a lottery held in London in 1767. The winners who accepted the parcels of land agreed to pay rent on them and to settle them within 10 years. Two years later, in 1769, the island's new owners persuaded the British government to let the island become a separate colony, distinct from Nova Scotia. This was the first step in a century-long effort to establish the island as an independent province.

Also in 1769, William Patterson, one of the island's landowners, was appointed governor-in-chief of the island. When he left England to visit his new domain, Patterson was filled with optimism about the island's potential. Upon his arrival, however, he was shocked and disappointed to find that the other landlords had made almost no attempt to settle tenants in their townships. To make matters worse, the colony was almost destitute, because

Opposite: Potatoes were introduced to the island in the 1770s and soon became its most important crop. This picture of a potato harvest was taken in the 1920s.

few of the owners had been paying the rent or taxes they owed. On the other hand, Patterson found that many pioneers, including a number of poor Scottish farmers who had come to the New World seeking a better life, saw great opportunity on the island. But these tenant farmers had to pay steep rents or purchase fees to the landowners back in England, and many of them could not afford to do so. The hopeful settlers thus found themselves as poor and insecure as they had been back in Europe, and they soon began to resent the landlords. When a local government called the House of Assembly was formed in 1773, the uneasy relationship between landlords and tenants was frequently the topic of discussion.

Patterson went back to England to report the conditions on Isle St. John and stayed there for nearly five years, leaving the few thousand Scots and Acadians on the island to fend for themselves. At least four times, the island was attacked and raided by privateers from New England. Rebels against the British crown, these privateers needed food and other provisions to help them survive during the American Revolution. Patterson returned to his governorship in 1780.

The Land Question

For the next century or so, until the island became a member of the Dominion of Canada in 1873, the central issue of life on the island concerned the land. Who should own it? How should settlement take place? Who should have the final say over land use, the settlers who worked the land or the owners in England and Scotland?

One crisis occurred when the American Revolution ended. Hundreds of British Loyalists fled from the newly independent United States. Some of them arrived on the island, looking for land to call their own. Without consulting the British government or the absentee landowners, Governor Patterson seized property on which rent was owed and sold it to the Loyalists. This act of defiance caused an uproar among the landowners back in England and Scotland and forced Patterson out of office.

In 1799, the British government changed the name of Isle St. John to Prince Edward Island in honor of King George III's son Edward. Around the same time, settlers—mostly Scottish farming families—continued to arrive to populate the island. The land was cleared for agriculture, and prosperous fishing villages sprang up along the coast. By the early 1800s, the island was producing enough potatoes, vegetables, and fish to export some of its bounty to neighboring provinces. The population of the province more than tripled during the middle of the 19th century, increasing from 22,000 in 1827 to 72,000 in 1855. By this time, Prince Edward Island had become the most densely populated colony in British North America.

The chamber where the delegates to the Charlottetown Conference met in September 1864 has been preserved as a monument to the meeting that was the birthplace of a united Canadian nation.

As the island's fortune increased, so did the residents' demands to own the property on which they lived and worked. Insisting that those who tilled the land had the right to own it, the tenants grew more and more aggressive toward the landlords. Island politics were dominated by this issue, and party lines were drawn between those who favored tenants' rights to own property and those who supported the landlords' claims.

A turning point in island affairs came in 1859, when the Crown gave the island government permission to buy up the claims of some of the landowners who owed rent and sell the land to deserving and responsible settlers. Unfortunately, the House of Assembly did not have enough money to buy much of the available land. The island asked the British government for a loan, and the request was refused. This brought the land question to a climax. An angry mob of impatient tenants marched on Charlottetown, causing a riot. British troops had to be called in from Halifax, Nova Scotia, to restore order. A year later, the British government set up a commission to investigate the land question. Although the commission recommended that tenants be given the right to own the land, its report was rejected by both the powerful landlords and the colonial administrators of the British government.

Confederation

In the meantime, British colonies throughout Canada were growing rapidly. These colonies were eager to increase and consolidate their strength and wealth; they also wanted to protect themselves from their powerful neighbor to the south, the United States, which harbored ambitions toward acquiring some Canadian territory. Many Canadians felt that the colonies should join together to form a confederation of provinces. The two large colonies called Canada West (now Ontario) and Canada East (now Quebec) had already joined together; the maritime colonies of New Brunswick, Nova Scotia, and Prince Edward Island were considering a union of their own.

Prince Edward Islanders, however, rejected the idea of confederation. They felt that they were doing quite well without help from either the home government in England or the other British North American colonies. Most islanders thought that the only reason to join with the other colonies would be to have access to enough money to buy out all of the absentee landlords. And because the other maritime colonies were as destitute as the island, the people of Prince Edward Island decided there would be no advantage in giving up their independence.

In 1864, Nova Scotia once again tried to persuade the island to join a maritime union. A meeting of representatives from the various colonies was planned. Trying to win the interest of the islanders, the planners offered to hold the meeting in Charlottetown. The Charlottetown Conference of September 1864 did not cause much of a stir among the islanders, who were far more excited about a traveling circus that happened to be visiting the island at the time. Nevertheless, it brought together representatives of the maritime colonies and the mainland colonies. After more than a week of discussions and speeches, the delegates had decided that all the provinces should confederate, or join together, to form a Canadian nation, and they had even begun discussing the future constitution of the country. The only colony that was still not interested in the idea of confederation was the host of the conference, Prince Edward Island.

The islanders' enthusiasm increased somewhat when Canada West and Canada East promised to give the island a large sum of money to buy out the absentee landlords. Later, however, this offer was withdrawn at another conference in Quebec, and the islanders decided they had nothing to gain by joining the confederation. Therefore, in 1867, when the rest of the British colonies confederated to form a new union called the Dominion of Canada, Prince Edward Island did not join them.

Within a few years, worsening economic conditions on Prince Edward Island forced the islanders to reconsider. Many historians feel that the Dominion, anxious to bring the island into its fold, was responsible for at least some of these problems. For example, the Dominion undermined a promising trade agreement between Prince Edward Island and the United States by threatening the island with economic sanctions—that is, with higher prices on goods bought from the Dominion and steep export taxes on products exported to the Dominion from the island.

The island's economy began to languish. Then, when a plan to build a railroad across the island nearly bankrupted the colony, the Canadian government refused to help unless the island joined the Dominion. So, in April 1873, the people of Prince Edward Island voted on their future. One choice was higher taxes to prop up their crippled economy; the other choice was confederation. They chose confederation. On July 1, 1873, Prince Edward Island became part of the Dominion of Canada. Many islanders were dismayed by this turn of events, but they quickly saw the advantage of confederation when the federal government gave its new province enough money to settle the land question once and for all. The island government finally purchased all the land that was owned by absentee landlords and resold it to the residents.

Shipbuilders at work on the vessel *Victory Chimes* in 1918. Once an important island industry, shipbuilding no longer contributes to Prince Edward Island's economy.

The Island Province

Tiny in size and with the smallest population of all the Canadian provinces, Prince Edward Island has developed slowly and somewhat unsteadily in the years since confederation. During the 1880s and 1890s, the island's economy thrived on agriculture and shipbuilding, and its population rose to 110,000. But a number of factors caused a reversal of fortune for the island at the beginning of the 20th century, causing the population to diminish and the economy to stagnate.

Perhaps the most important factor in the decline of the island, and of the maritime provinces in general, was Canada's expansion in the west. As Canadians explored and settled the vast western portion of their nation, the focus of the national economy and politics shifted westward. Prince Edward Island could no longer compete with the output of much larger farms in the new prairie provinces of Alberta, Saskatchewan, and Manitoba, and the lure of jobs and land drew thousands of people away from the island to seek their fortunes in the west.

Prince Edward Island was at a disadvantage in yet another way. Because of its small population and its lack of mineral resources and energy sources, the Industrial Revolution that swept over North America during the 1880s completely bypassed the island. No large factories were built there to offer high wages, inexpensive consumer goods, or steady jobs.

Although its isolation, its small size, and its lack of resources have prevented Prince Edward Island from becoming a major economic force within Canada, these conditions have also allowed the island's traditions of independence and self-sufficiency to remain strong. When the Great Depression of the 1930s devastated much of the rest of the world, the island was able to hold its own. Although potato growers saw their income drop by some 75 percent during a 5-year period, the province was able to feed its people. In addition, many islanders have argued that Prince Edward Island's fresh, clean air and lack of overcrowding have more than made up for the hardships caused by the slow pace of its economy.

The islanders are debating whether or not to build a bridge or tunnel to the mainland. One plan calls for this bridge to be built across the Northumberland Strait.

During the 20th century, however, the island fell further and further behind the rest of the nation. Unemployment grew steadily worse, and social services, including health care and education, suffered because the provincial government did not have enough money to keep up with advances made elsewhere in the country. By the end of the 1960s, the island had decided to give up some of its cherished independence and to accept assistance from the federal government.

In 1969, an economic plan was devised to diversify the island's economy and to improve its residents' quality of life. The program included funds to help the unemployed, to promote the growth of small businesses, and to establish social service programs, such as comprehensive health insurance. The island's educational system and its schools were modernized as well, making them the equal of those elsewhere in the nation. Attempts to diversify the economy met with less success. The old problems—especially the difficulty of access to the island and the high cost of

energy—once again prevented any large-scale manufacturing ventures. Agriculture remains the island's chief source of income. Jobs in government agencies and offices have increased dramatically and are another important component of the island economy. More than 12 percent of the island's workers hold government jobs.

Federal intervention has certainly raised the island's standard of living, but it has also created a dependence on federal funds to fuel the local economy. As the province heads into the 1990s and beyond, its residents are faced with a number of pressing issues: How dependent on the federal government should the island be? How can the island retain its natural beauty while at the same time profit from tourism? How can it play a greater role in the politics and economy of both the nation and the maritime region? This province of 126,646 determined people, reveling in their island's beauty and bounty, will no doubt face these issues with a characteristically independent and persevering spirit.

The Economy

More than 60,000 men and women work on Prince Edward Island, struggling to strengthen and diversify their economy. Unemployment hovers at around 10 percent, and personal income is about 75 percent of the national average. Despite these discouraging statistics, most islanders remain passionately devoted to their homes and their way of life.

Three factors have kept the island's economy relatively stagnant. These factors are the small population, the island's lack of an inexpensive energy source, and the high cost of transporting goods to and from the mainland. Electrical energy on the island is the most expensive in Canada. Without enough fresh water to generate hydroelectricity, the island is completely dependent on imported oil, and the high cost of this commodity prohibits large-scale manufacturing. Efforts are being made to explore alternative sources of energy, including wind and solar power.

The issue of transportation is a matter of deep concern to island residents. Travel within the island is relatively easy; a system of about 3,400 miles (5,440 kilometers) of highways gives

Opposite: An oyster fisherman rakes shellfish from the seafloor. Prince Edward Island oysters, especially those from Malpeque Bay on the north coast, are highly prized by seafood lovers.
Above: Ferries such as the 900-passenger *Abegweit* are the principal means of travel to and from the island. Air service also reaches Prince Edward Island, and plans are under way to build a bridge or tunnel linking the island with the mainland.

Agriculture has always been central to the island's economy, but the number of small farms is decreasing as fewer and fewer farmers work larger and larger parcels of land.

residents and tourists access to even the most isolated inlets on the island. Getting to and from the mainland, however, is another matter. Cape Tormentine, New Brunswick, about 9 miles (15 kilometers) across the Northumberland Strait from Port Borden, Prince Edward Island, is the mainland's nearest point. A ferry service operated by the federal transportation company, Canadian National (CN), transports people and goods across the strait throughout the year. Often during the winter, however, the strait ices over, which means that the ferries cannot move until icebreakers clear the passage. Another ferry service, a private com-

pany called Northumberland Ferries, operates between Wood's Island, Prince Edward Island, and Caribou, Nova Scotia, from April to November. In addition, Eastern Provincial Airways and Air Canada offer daily flights between the island and several Canadian cities.

The air and ferry services are efficient, but many people think that the island needs a less expensive, more reliable connection to the mainland. A tunnel or bridge across the Northumberland Strait would allow trucks to carry goods to and from the island and would also make it easier for visitors to reach Prince Edward Island. Some islanders are fiercely opposed to the idea of a direct link with the mainland; they feel that preserving the island's characteristic independence and solitude is well worth the economic costs of isolation. But when islanders cast their ballots on this issue in the summer of 1990, a majority of them favored a fixed connection of some sort with the mainland. Plans are now under way to build a bridge or tunnel to New Brunswick, although environmental concerns about disturbing a valuable lobster habitat or upsetting the tides in the strait may interfere.

In the meantime, the island's economy focuses on agriculture, fishing, and tourism. Whether or not the mainland connection is built, these three industries are likely to remain the backbone of Prince Edward Island's economy.

Agriculture

Prince Edward Island lives up to its nickname, the Garden of Canada. More than half of the island's territory is farmland—a larger proportion of farmland than any other province in Canada.

Prince Edward Island's main crop is the potato, earning the province its other nickname, Spud Island. The roots of this island specialty are deep; islanders have been growing potatoes since the 1770s. Later, especially after Irish settlers arrived during the 1830s, the crop grew in importance. Potatoes of all kinds flourish in the island's soil and climate. Most important are seed potatoes, varieties of potatoes grown not to eat but to seed fields in other

Opposite: The island has about 1,000 dairy farms.

provinces and countries. The first crop of seed potatoes to be exported from Canada was produced on Spud Island in 1918. By the 1980s, about 30 percent of the total potato-field acreage was being used to grow seed potatoes. Together with the province of New Brunswick, Prince Edward Island produces nearly 90 percent of Canada's total seed-potato exports.

Forty-five percent of the potatoes grown on Prince Edward Island are grown for consumption. Among the island's 32 varieties of potatoes, the late-maturing, red-skinned Sebago is best for boiling and mashing; the Russet Burbank, for baking and for french fries. The remaining 25 percent of the island's potatoes are also used to make potato chips, instant potatoes, and other processed products that are fast becoming an important part of Prince Edward Island's agricultural planning.

However, many agricultural experts have long warned islanders about the dangers of relying on just one crop. Island farmers are now adding peas, turnips, broccoli, and cauliflower to their harvests, finding that these crops yield more value per acre than potatoes and in addition draw fewer nutrients out of the soil. Tobacco is another island crop that is profitable and easy to grow; about 2,500 tons of it are harvested every year.

One thousand dairy farms, with a total of 22,000 dairy cows, produce about 106 million quarts (100 million liters) of milk every year, adding $30 million to the provincial economy. Cattle are also raised for beef, for earnings of about $35 million annually.

Island agriculture has changed in recent years, with a shrinking number of farmers working on increasingly larger farms. In 1951, more than 10,000 farmers tilled the soil on Prince Edward Island, but in 1986 only about 2,800 islanders owned farms. During the same period, the size of individual farms more than doubled, from 108 acres (44 hectares) to 237 acres (96 hectares).

Fishing

The waters around Prince Edward Island contain an abundance and variety of fish unsurpassed in Canada, making the island a

Tourism plays an ever-greater role in Prince Edward Island's economy. Mild summers, warm waters, and local delicacies such as lobster help attract about 700,000 visitors each year.

haven for both commercial and sport fishing. More than 3,000 fishermen ply the island's waters, adding more than $36 million to the provincial economy every year.

Lobsters have long been one of Prince Edward Island's prime resources; by 1900, lobsters accounted for half of the annual catch, and by 1990 they had become by far the most valuable marine species to be harvested. About 5,500 tons of lobsters are caught each year. Many of the lobsters are transported to Nova Scotia and New Brunswick by ship and then sent on by rail to other markets. Not all of these delicious shellfish are exported, however. Lobster suppers are one of Prince Edward Island's most

enduring traditions. Throughout the summer, towns across the island sponsor these shellfish feasts for residents and tourists alike.

Another Prince Edward Island speciality is the Malpeque oyster. Named for the Malpeque Bay on the northwest corner of Prince County, these oysters are appreciated all over the world. More than 10 million of them are harvested annually, and together with the island's equally succulent scallops, they bring in about $4 million each year.

Prince Edward Island's marine bounty does not end with shellfish. Even before the largest bluefin tuna ever caught—weighing in at 1,496 pounds (680 kilograms)—was landed off the island's northeast coast in 1979, sportsmen and commercial fishermen flocked to this region, eager to do battle with tuna and other challenging open-water fish. Groundfish, such as cod, hake, flounder, and redfish, are also caught.

Tourism

Attracting visitors to the island has become increasingly important to the provincial economy. More than 700,000 tourists add about $60 million to Prince Edward Island's economy each year. Both the federal and provincial governments are working to further promote the island's natural beauty, activities, and accommodations. But the tourist season is quite short, limited to about 8 to 10 weeks during the summer. Winter activities, such as hockey and curling, have never been as popular with tourists as swimming and sunbathing in the warm summer months.

The future of the economy will depend, as always, on the tenacity and perseverance of the islanders. Balancing the need for tourist dollars against the disruption of their solitary life-style is just one of the challenges facing Prince Edward Islanders in the 1990s.

The People

With 126,646 inhabitants, Prince Edward Island has the smallest population of any Canadian province. Its people make up only half of one percent of the national population. It also has one of the most rural populations in North America. Fewer than 37 percent of the islanders live in Prince Edward Island's only city, Charlottetown, in the smaller town of Summerside, or in their suburbs. Most of the other islanders live in tiny fishing villages on the coast or in farming communities in the interior. Because the island is so narrow, no one lives farther than 16 miles (25.6 kilometers) from the sea.

Prince Edward Island has the most culturally homogeneous population in Canada—that is, a greater percentage of its inhabitants share a common ethnic background than is the case in any other province. Nearly 80 percent of Prince Edward Island residents trace their heritage back to the British Isles. They are, however, proud to identify with the specific part of Britain from which their ancestors hailed. Descendants of settlers from Scotland have their own heritage and traditions, as do the Irish and

Opposite: This man is a resident of Murray Harbour on the eastern edge of the island. The majority of Prince Edward Island's inhabitants live in the countryside or in small villages such as Murray Harbour.
Above: Musicians at an Irish festival celebrate Ireland's contribution to the island's population and culture. Each of Prince Edward Island's ethnic groups holds its own fairs and festivals every year.

the English. Each of these subgroups of the British population has added its own influences to the island culture, which includes Scottish highland dancing, Irish folk singing, and English architecture.

The Acadians are an important minority. Most of the 10,000 descendants of the Acadian settlers live in Prince County, where they account for nearly 25 percent of the population. They have had to struggle to keep their language and traditions alive, often through years of discrimination, but their striking log houses, distinctive crafts and cooking, and unique French dialect are testimony to the remarkable endurance of the Acadian culture.

Also residing in Prince County are some 400 Micmacs, descendants of the island's first inhabitants. Approximately 55 Micmac families now live in a reserve on Lennox Island, on the

Performers at an Acadian festival, wearing traditional clothing, dance an old-time step. The Acadian language, a dialect based on French, remains alive in Prince County.

At a branch of Holland College in Summerside, mastering a computerized geographic information system is part of a training program in urban and rural planning. The system contains information that can be used to plan mining, forestry, and land-use projects throughout the maritime provinces.

edge of Malpeque Bay on the north shore, where the British set-tlers pushed them during the late 19th century. The Micmacs of Prince Edward Island were the first Native Americans to be Christianized in Canada, and St. Anne's Church, built in 1895 on Lennox Island, commemorates that fact.

Education and Culture

By the 1960s, a profound lack of funds on Prince Edward Island meant that the province was spending less on education than any other Canadian province. Although schools, along with churches, provided social focuses for their community, the educational stan-dards were nevertheless deplorably low. During the 1970s and 1980s, with money and administrative help from the federal gov-ernment, Prince Edward Island's educational system underwent revolutionary change.

During the 1970s, boosted by an influx of federal capital, teachers' salaries increased, school systems were consolidated, buildings and supplies were improved, and higher teaching stan-dards, including the requirement of a university degree, were put in force. Long gone are the one-room schoolhouses that peppered the island into the 1950s. By 1990, the province was spending

Robert Harris's *Fathers of Confederation* hangs in the gallery of the Confederation Center in Charlottetown.

some $90 million dollars each year on its 70 schools. About 26,000 children attended these schools, which were comparable in quality with those elsewhere in Canada.

Two institutions of higher learning are located on the island. The University of Prince Edward Island was created in 1969 by the merging of two schools, Prince of Wales College, which had been founded in 1834, and St. Dunstan's College, which had been founded in 1855. The university is located in Charlottetown and enrolls about 1,800 students in undergraduate programs in the arts, sciences, and business. Plans are being made to introduce a degree program in veterinary medicine at the university; it will be the first in the maritime provinces. Holland College was created as part of the federal government's plan to increase educational opportunities for islanders. It has campuses in several places throughout the province and offers a wide range of vocational and occupational programs.

The provincial government has a Department of Community and Cultural Affairs that works with artists and cultural historians to protect and enhance the arts and artifacts of the island, which are displayed in museums and galleries across the province. Another important cultural institution is the Prince Edward Island Museum and Heritage Foundation, which administers the island's many historical landmarks and collects and interprets new information about Acadian, Micmac, and British culture.

The performing arts also flourish in the province. Small theaters feature dramas and musicals, especially during the summer months. The cultural center of the island is the Confederation Center of the Arts in Charlottetown. Built in 1964 to commemorate the 100th anniversary of the Charlottetown Conference, this architectural masterpiece covers two downtown blocks and contains a memorial hall, a theater, an art gallery, a museum, and the provincial library.

The Confederation Center art gallery is one of Canada's best museums. Not only does it have a fine permanent collection of work by provincial and international artists, but it hosts traveling exhibits from around the world. One highlight of the museum is a collection of masterpieces by Robert Harris, Prince Edward Island's most accomplished painter. Born in Wales, Harris arrived on the island in 1865 at the age of seven. He became one of Canada's leading portrait artists, but his best-known work is *The Fathers of Confederation*, a re-creation of the Charlottetown Conference of 1864.

Without a doubt, however, the most popular attraction of the Confederation Center of the Arts is the longest-running musical play in Canadian history: *Anne of Green Gables*, based on the novel of the same name by Lucy Maud Montgomery. That novel was published in 1908 and is probably Prince Edward Island's most famous export. It has been been translated into 16 languages and made into two television series that have been broadcast around the world.

The book's spunky heroine is Anne Shirley, an orphan girl who is adopted by a farming family on Prince Edward Island. Anne falls in love with her new island home and, in turn, melts the hearts of even the most solitary and unsociable islanders. Lucy Maud Montgomery (1874–1942), the author of *Anne of Green Gables* and its seven sequels, was born and brought up on the island, and Prince Edward Island's magnificent landscapes inspired her throughout her prolific career. She wrote 22 novels and dozens of short stories and poems, but only two of her works are set off the island. "We Prince Edward Islanders are a loyal race," she once wrote. "In our secret soul, we believe that there is no place like the little Province that gave us birth. We may suspect that it isn't quite perfect, any more than any other place on this planet, but you will not catch us admitting it. And how furiously we hate any one who does say it!"

Anne of Green Gables and her creator are honored throughout the island, but especially in the town of Cavendish, on the north coast. Montgomery was raised by her grandparents in this Queens County farming community, and Cavendish provided her with the setting for much of her fiction. Visitors from all over the world come to see the farmhouse called Green Gables, now a museum located in Prince Edward Island National Park. Montgomery's grandparents' home has been converted into the Green Gables post office, and other sites that are described in the book, such as Anne's Babbling Brook, the Haunted Woods, and Lovers' Lane, are also commemorated with plaques and monuments. Lucy Maud Montgomery is buried in Cavendish Cemetery.

Sports and Recreation

Prince Edward Island has no professional sports teams, but amateur athletics of all kinds are practiced on the island. Hockey and curling, two of Canada's favorite sports, are nowhere more popular than on Prince Edward Island. With more than 20 indoor rinks, the island is well equipped for hockey play and practice. Many professional hockey players have come from Prince Edward Island, including Gerard Gallant of the National Hockey League (NHL).

Another popular sport played on the ice is curling. Second only to hockey in popularity, curling draws thousands of devoted

Water sports are very popular on Prince Edward Island during the summer, perhaps because the Gulf of St. Lawrence and the Northumberland Strait are warmer than the Atlantic Ocean off the shores of nearby New England.

fans on the island. Introduced to Prince Edward Island in the 1920s, curling involves propelling granite stones along a 138-foot (42-meter) lane of ice. Players compete to see who can hit, or get nearest to, a target stone at the other end of the lane. Enthusiasm for the game, which is Scottish in origin, grew during the 1960s and 1970s, and in 1977 a group of Charlottetown players won the men's junior world championship.

During the summer, softball is the most popular team sport, but most islanders are content to enjoy the outdoors without competing. Swimming and boating in the island's warm waters, sunbathing on the sandy beaches, and fishing in the Gulf of St. Lawrence are just a few of the pastimes enjoyed by residents and tourists alike. The island also has 10 golf courses, a number of amusement parks, and plenty of facilities for riding horseback, camping, bird-watching, and hiking. It is scheduled to host the Canada Games—the nation's premier amateur athletic event—in 1991, so it is likely that even more tourists than usual will visit the island that summer.

The Communities

Charlottetown and Queens County

Just as Prince Edward Island is both the smallest province in Canada and one of the most beautiful, Charlottetown is the smallest and one of the most charming of the provincial capitals. With just 16,000 residents, Charlottetown has none of the drawbacks of big-city life: no polluting smokestacks, no overcrowded or littered streets. Yet it offers many of the benefits of urban living. Charlottetown is not only the island's seat of government but its cultural and educational center, its chief port, and its shopping and banking hub.

The only city on Prince Edward Island, Charlottetown is situated on a broad harbor opening into the Northumberland Strait. Three small rivers join to form the harbor, so that almost every point in and around Charlottetown has a river view. Although the city was not officially incorporated until 1855, settlement began in the area in the early 1700s, when the French built Port La Joye on one of the arms of the harbor. When the British took control of the island in 1758, they renamed this outpost Fort Amherst. Six years later, when Captain Samuel Holland arrived to survey the island, he and fellow Englishman Charles Morris chose the site for Charlottetown.

Opposite: This double-decker bus offers a tour of Charlottetown, the province's capital.
Above: The city is small enough that it can be seen in the course of an afternoon walk, as this aerial view shows.

During the next century, the village that had originally had fewer than 100 inhabitants grew into a bustling city. Acadians, English, Irish, and Scots arrived in Charlottetown by the hundreds. When the city was chosen as the site of the Confederation Conference of 1864, its importance as a colonial capital was reinforced. By the time Prince Edward Island joined the Dominion of Canada in 1873, the new provincial capital was the 11th largest city in Canada. And when the 20th century dawned, Charlottetown was fully equipped to fulfill its role as the island's cultural and political center: It had modern water and sewer services, electric streetlights, hospitals, schools, and, most important, a railroad station and a full-service port.

Today the city is home to the province's major cultural and educational institutions as well as to its government and commercial offices. The Confederation Center of the Arts is one of the leading cultural centers of the maritime provinces, and the University of Prince Edward Island attracts students from throughout Canada.

At the southernmost tip of the city is Victoria Park. One of the province's oldest structures, the old Government House, built in 1834, is located there; it is the official residence of the prov-

Victoria Park, named for Queen Victoria of Great Britain, is one of the landmarks of the capital.

ince's lieutenant governor. Across the street is Beaconsfield, a Victorian home, built in 1877, that houses the Prince Edward Island Museum and Heritage Foundation offices, the Center of Genealogical Research, and a bookstore specializing in island history.

Most of the city's residents work for the government, although many find employment in industrial food processing plants and clothing factories. Tourism is the city's fastest-growing economic activity; indeed, as the capital of Prince Edward Island, Charlottetown welcomes some 600,000 to 700,000 visitors every year.

Charlottetown is located in Queens County, the island's central region. Circling Queens County is Blue Heron Drive, one of the island's three scenic highways. Approximately 114 miles (183 kilometers) long, Blue Heron Drive passes through farmland, along the white sandy beaches of the coast, and through Prince Edward Island National Park to the town of Cavendish, depicted in *Anne of Green Gables*.

St. Peters, tucked away at the head of an inlet on the northwest shore, is typical of the many tiny fishing villages that dot the island's coastline.

Because of catches such as this one, the people of North Lake call their town the Tuna Fishing Capital of the World.

Summerside and Prince County

Located near the head of Bedeque Bay on the province's southern shore, Summerside is about 37 miles (60 kilometers) west of Charlottetown in Prince County. With more than 7,500 people, Summerside is second only to the capital in terms of population and is the only other town with more than 2,000 people on the island.

The western region of Prince Edward Island was inhabited by Micmac Indians when French settlers arrived in the mid-18th century. Later, after the British began arriving in the late 18th century, the village of Green's Shore arose on the present-day site of Summerside. It developed into a major shipbuilding center. In 1840, the town's first inn, called Summerside House, was built; a few years later, the villagers officially changed their town's name to Summerside. After the demise of the shipbuilding trade at the beginning of the 20th century, Summerside's economy focused on agriculture, especially potatoes and dairy products. In addition, during the 1910s and 1920s, Summerside was the center of Prince Edward Island's foray into the fur-trading business. Two enterprising young fur trappers began breeding silver foxes in captivity and made a fortune selling their furs until the market collapsed in the Great Depression of the 1930s. Since then, Summerside, like the rest of the province, has depended on farming, fishing, and tourism to fuel its economy. It remains the island's principal port for potato shipments.

The country around Summerside has some of the most beautiful scenery on the island. North of the town is Malpeque Bay, a large body of water that nearly cuts Prince Edward Island in two. The island's well-known Malpeque oysters are named for the bay, whose waters also provide seafood lovers with lobsters and scallops. But this region of Prince County has more than seafood to offer. Both the Micmac Indians and the Acadians were early settlers, and descendants of both groups still live in Prince County. Nearly 25 percent of the county's population is Acadian. The Acadian French dialect is still spoken, and an Acadian pioneer village is one of many historic recreations of traditional Acadian life. Prince County also has the island's only Acadian restaurant. Farther north, the Lennox Island Micmac Reserve is home to most of the island's Native American population, 400 or so descendants of the original small band of Micmac who came from Nova Scotia.

Kings County

Kings County occupies the eastern section of Prince Edward Island and has some of the most unspoiled landscape in the province. Its white sandy beaches are lined with red sandstone bluffs. Dozens of white-painted lighthouse towers that once lit the way to safe harbor for the island's fishermen still stand in commemoration of a bygone age of sailing ships.

Although there are no large towns in the region, several villages are noteworthy. Murray River and Murray Harbour were the site of a major shipbuilding center during the mid-1800s. Those days are gone, but the Handcraft Co-op Association of Murray River offers examples of the work of island craftspeople, including potters, weavers, woodworkers, and quilters. At Murray Harbour, the past comes alive at the Log Cabin Museum, which depicts 19th-century life with antique tools and equipment. At the northeastern tip of the island is the village of North Lake, which calls itself the Tuna Fishing Capital of the World and provides a harbor for both commercial fishing vessels and the thousands of sport fishermen who come to take on the giant bluefin tuna every fall. Next to North Lake is East Point, called by the Indians Kespemenagek, or "the east end of the island." The East Point lighthouse, built in 1867, is one of the island's three staffed lighthouses.

Things to Do and See

• **Confederation Center of the Arts,** Charlottetown: Drama, art, the provincial library, and a restaurant are found in this large cultural center.

• **House of International Dolls,** Dunstable: A collection of more than 1,800 dolls from around the world, featuring antique dolls, Mother Goose characters, and figures from literary works, is housed in this charming museum.

• **Fort Amherst/Port La Joye National Historic Park,** Rocky Point: The site of the first permanent European settlement on the island has an audiovisual presentation, a visitor information center, and picnic grounds.

• **Micmac Indian Village, Rocky Point:** One of a series of reconstructed villages celebrating the life of the Micmac Indians on P.E.I., this community displays artifacts and traditional lodgings.

• **Prince Edward Island Acquarium,** Stanley Bridge: Featuring numerous species of native fish, the aquarium includes oysters displayed in a re-created oyster bed. The Manor of Birds has more than 750 specimens of preserved birds, and the Hall of Butterflies displays butterflies from around the world.

Opposite: Trail riding—through woodlands and fields or along the beaches— is one way for visitors to see the island. *Above:* Near Tignish, in the northwest, Irish moss is farmed. The "moss" is really a type of red algae that is used as an ingredient in soaps, fertilizers, and other commercial materials

• **Elmira Railways Museum,** Elmira: Originally the eastern terminus of a railway system, this depot is now a museum tracing the history of the railroad on P.E.I.

• **Mill River Fun Park,** Woodstock: This amusement park has a grounded pirate ship, a number of water slides, miniature golf, a petting zoo, and a 650-seat outdoor amphitheater.

• **Victoria Park,** Charlottetown: This urban oasis contains the neoclassical Government House (the official residence of the island's lieutenant governor), together with expansive harbor views, a grassy park, and a public swimming pool and play area.

• **Prince Edward Island National Park,** Cavendish: One of the smallest but most popular Canadian parks stretches for 25 miles (40 kilometers) along the north shore of the island. The dunes at Blooming Point at the park's eastern edge have grown to a height of 75 feet (25 meters). The park features three campgrounds, a tent site, swimming beaches, and a golf course.

Among the many plants exhibited at Malpeque Gardens in Prince County are 600 different varieties of dahlias.

Old-time music reigns at the Fiddling Festival at Rollo Bay.

• **Anne of Green Gables Museum** at Silver Bush, Park Corner: The home of Lucy Maud Montgomery's uncle, whom she often visited, and its environs provide some of the settings for the *Anne of Green Gables* series of books. A craft shop is located on the site.

• **Acadian Museum of Prince Edward Island,** Summerside: Photographs and artifacts illustrating the history of Acadians on the island are displayed in the museum's main gallery. The display includes a photograph of Stanislas-F. Poirier, who in 1854 became the first Acadian elected to the Legislative Assembly.

• **Malpeque Gardens,** Malpeque: Features 600 different varieties of dahlias, prizewinning begonias, and two rose gardens. A wooden arch opens onto the Anne of Green Gables Gardens, where quotations from the novel are placed along flower-lined paths.

• **Buffaloland Provincial Park,** Milltown Cross: Herds of North American buffalo and white-tailed deer in a 100-acre (40-hectare) enclosure.

Festivals & Holidays

Throughout the summer, residents and tourists alike feast on crustaceans such as these at lobster suppers.

Winter: Every year in late November, Prince Edward Islanders get in the Christmas mood at the **Crafts Council Annual Christmas Fair,** in Charlottetown, where fine arts and crafts created by native and international artists are for sale. Then, in December, the **Santa Claus Parade** in Souris delights children and adults alike. Towns and villages across the maritime provinces celebrate winter carnivals. One of the biggest and best is the **Charlottetown Winter Carnival** in February. Harness racing, skiing and skating competitions, and a Winter Carnival Ball take the chill out of the long island winters.

Spring: Every April, one of Canada's favorite sports comes to the island for its most competitive event during the **Canadian Curling Championships,** held in Summerside at the Silver Fox Curling and Yacht Club.

Summer: **The Charlottetown Festival,** held every year at the Confederation Center of the Arts in Charlottetown, presents theater productions throughout the summer, including the beloved *Anne of Green Gables.* P.E.I.'s Irish residents celebrate their heritage during the **Irish Moss Festival** at the beginning of July at Tignish, with the Miss Irish Moss pageant, parades, dances, fireworks, and harness racing. On July 1, P.E.I. joins the rest of Canada in celebrating the nation's birth on **Canada Day** with parades, races, games, fireworks, and other events in towns and villages throughout the province. The island's most important crop is honored during the **Potato Blossom Festival** in O'Leary; a Miss Potato Blossom is crowned, and horse racing, concerts, and a formal banquet and dance take place. Scotland comes to P.E.I. in August during the **Annual Highland Games** in Alden and at the **Outdoor Scottish Fiddle and Dance Festival** at Richmond. Tyne Valley in the north celebrates one of the island's most valuable assets at the **Oyster Festival.** A lobster supper, special dances, and a horse-pulling competition highlight the **Fête Acadienne de la Région Evangeline,** focusing on the special contribution of the Acadians to the island. The **Festival Acadian and Agricultural Exhibition** in Abram Village features concerts, Acadian handicrafts, and a live-stock exhibition. **Old Home Week** in Charlottetown at the end of August features one of Canada's most popular rural fairs.

Fall: The **Prince Edward Island Festival of the Arts** gets autumn off to a spectacular start with more than 100 province-wide events. The Orwell Corner Historic Village in Queens County hosts the **Harvest Home Festival** in October, featuring games, entertainment, threshing demonstrations, and cider pressing.

Prince Edward Island's economic future will involve a balancing act between the desire to profit from tourism and the need to preserve the island's natural beauty and unspoiled charm.

Chronology

1534   French explorer Jacques Cartier lands on the island, which is inhabited by the Micmac.

1719   French settlers arrive. The island is named Ile St. Jean.

1755   French Acadians arrive after expulsion from Nova Scotia.

1758   The British win control of the island from France and deport most of the Acadians. The island is renamed Isle St. John.

1771   Potatoes are grown for the first time on the island.

1770s   Raiders from the present-day United States attack the island several times.

1799   Isle St. John is renamed Prince Edward Island. Over the following decades, it is settled by Scottish, Irish, and English emigrants, although the question of land ownership remains politically troublesome for years.

1864   The Charlottetown Conference is the birthplace of a united Dominion of Canada.

1873   P.E.I. becomes part of the Dominion of Canada.

1908   The novel *Anne of Green Gables,* by Lucy Maud Montgomery, is published.

1964   The Confederation Center of the Arts opens in Charlottetown.

1989   The 125th anniversary of the Charlottetown Conference is celebrated.

1991   P.E.I. hosts the Canada Games.

Further Reading

Bolger, Francis W., et al. *Spirit of Place: Lucy Maud Montgomery and Prince Edward Island*. New York: Oxford University Press, 1983.

Bumsted, J. M. *Land, Settlement, and Politics in Eighteenth-Century Prince Edward Island*. Toronto: McGill–Queens University Press, 1987.

Clark, Andrew Hill. *Three Centuries and the Island*. Toronto: University of Toronto Press, 1959.

Fingard, Judith. *Jack in Port: Sailortowns of Eastern Canada*. Toronto: University of Toronto Press, 1982.

Frideres, James. *Canada's Indians: Contemporary Conflicts*. Englewood Cliffs, NJ: Prentice-Hall, 1974.

Hocking, Anthony. *Prince Edward Island*. Toronto and New York: McGraw-Hill Ryerson, 1978.

Holbrook, Sabra. *Canada's Kids*. New York: Atheneum, 1983.

Law, Kevin. *Canada*. New York: Chelsea House, 1990.

Lord, Margaret G., and Evelyn J. Macleod. *One Woman's Charlottetown: Diaries of Margaret Gray Lord, 1863, 1876, 1890*. Chicago: University of Chicago Press, 1988.

McNaught, Kenneth. *The Penguin History of Canada*. New York: Penguin, 1988.

Malcolm, Andrew. *The Canadians*. New York: Random House, 1985.

Meacham, J. H. *Illustrated Historical Atlas of Prince Edward Island*. Facsimile of 1880 edition. Belleville, Ontario: Mika Silk Screening, 1990.

Montgomery, Lucy Maud. *Anne of Green Gables*. New York: Bantam Books, 1976.

Rothe, Robert. *Acadia: The Story Behind the Scenery*. Las Vegas: KC Publications, 1979.

Wansbrough, M. B. *Great Canadian Lives*. New York: Doubleday, 1986.

Index

ACKNOWLEDGMENTS

Bettmann/Hulton: p. 14; The Bettmann Archive: pp. 17, 23; Diana Blume: p. 6; Canadian Consulate General: cover, pp. 3, 5, 8, 31, 32, 36, 38, 40, 42, 45, 46, 49, 55, 56, 57, 58; Holland College, Prince Edward Island, Canada: p. 41; Marine Atlantic: p. 12; National Archives of Canada/PA43964: p. 20; Northumberland Strait Crossing Project: pp. 28–29; Prince Edward Island Department of Tourism and Parks: p. 39; Prince Edward Island Department of Tourism and Parks/Barrett and MacKay: pp. 9, 30, 52, 54, 59; Prince Edward Island Department of Tourism and Parks/Kenneth Ginn: pp. 35, 51; Prince Edward Island Department of Tourism and Parks/J. Sylvester: p. 50; Prince Edward Island Public Archives and Records Office: pp. 15 (Accession #3466/72.66.1.8), 19 (Accession #2320/60–4), 26; Joe Roman: p. 48; Debora Smith: pp. 7, 11; John Sylvester/Holland College: p. 18

Suzanne LeVert has contributed several volumes to Chelsea House's LET'S DISCOVER CANADA series. She is the author of four previous books for young readers. One of these, *The Sakharov File*, biography of noted Russian physicist Andrei Sakharov, was selected as a Notable Book by the National Council for the Social Studies. Her other books include *AIDS: In Search of a Killer, The Doubleday Book of Famous Americans*, and *New York*. Ms. LeVert also has extensive experience as an editor, first in children's books at Simon & Schuster, then as associate editor at *Trialogue*, the magazine of the Trilateral Commission, and as senior editor at Save the Children, the international relief and development organization. She lives in Cambridge, Massachusetts.

George Sheppard, General Editor, is a lecturer on Canadian and American history at McMaster University in Hamilton, Ontario. Dr. Sheppard holds an honors B.A. and an M.A. in history from Laurentian University and earned his Ph.D. in Canadian history at McMaster. He has taught Canadian history at Nipissing University in North Bay. His research specialty is the War of 1812, and he has published articles in *Histoire sociale/Social History, Papers of the Bibliographical Society of Canada*, and *Ontario History*. Dr. Sheppard is a native of Timmins, Ontario.

Pierre Berton, Senior Consulting Editor, is the author of 34 books, including *The Mysterious North, Klondike, Great Canadians, The Last Spike, The Great Railway Illustrated, Hollywood's Canada, My Country: The Remarkable Past, The Wild Frontier, The Invasion of Canada, Why We Act Like Canadians, The Klondike Quest*, and *The Arctic Grail*. He has won three Governor General's Awards for creative nonfiction, two National Newspaper Awards, and two ACTRA "Nellies" for broadcasting. He is a Companion of the Order of Canada, a member of the Canadian News Hall of Fame, and holds 12 honorary degrees. Raised in the Yukon, Mr. Berton began his newspaper career in Vancouver. He then became managing editor of *McLean's*, Canada's largest magazine, and subsequently worked for the Canadian Broadcasting Network and the *Toronto Star*. He lives in Kleinburg, Ontario.